Creative Crafts for Kids

Back-to-School CRAFTS

By Sue Locke

Gareth Stevens
Publishing

Please visit our Web site www.garethstevens.com. For a free color catalog of all our high-quality books, call toll free 1-800-542-2595 or fax 1-877-542-2596.

Library of Congress Cataloging-in-Publication Data
Locke, Sue.
　　Back-to-school crafts / Sue Locke.
　　　　p. cm. --　(Creative crafts for kids)
　　Includes index.
　　ISBN 978-1-4339-3542-8 (lib. bdg.) -- ISBN 978-1-4339-3544-2 (pbk.)
　　ISBN 978-1-4339-3545-9 (6-pack)
　　1.　Handicraft--Juvenile literature.　I. Title.
　TT171.L63 2010
　745.5--dc22
　　　　　　　　　　　　　　　　　　　　2009037143　2009039233

Published in 2010 by
Gareth Stevens Publishing
111 East 14th Street, Suite 349
New York, NY 10003

© 2010 The Brown Reference Group Ltd.

For Gareth Stevens Publishing:
Art Direction: Haley Harasymiw
Editorial Direction: Kerri O'Donnell

For The Brown Reference Group Ltd:
Editorial Director: Lindsey Lowe
Managing Editor: Tim Harris
Children's Publisher: Anne O'Daly
Design Manager: David Poole
Production Director: Alastair Gourlay

Picture Credits:
All photographs: Martin Norris
Front Cover: Shutterstock: Lunetskaya and Martin Norris

Manufactured in the United States of America
1 2 3 4 5 6 7 8 9　12 11 10

CPSIA compliance information: Batch #BRW0102GS: For further information contact Gareth Stevens, New York, New York at 1-800-542-2595.

Contents

Introduction

Here are twelve fun and simple projects to fill the last few days of the school vacation. There are brilliant ideas for organizing you and your bedroom for the new term—make a holder for hair bands, a fab folder with a rain-forest game, and a handy tube for carrying home your artwork. The step-by-step photographs show you how it's all done!

YOU WILL NEED

Each project includes a list of all the things you need.

Before you buy new materials, look at home to see what you could use instead. For example, you can use an old piece of fabric such as a pillow case for the school days chart and empty candy tubes to make the pots for pens. Please remember to ask an adult before taking anything to use in your projects.

You can buy other items such as felt, craft foam, and a mug tree at department stores or craft shops.

Getting started

Read the steps for the project first.

Gather together all the items you need.

Cover your work surface with newspaper.

Wear an apron, or change into old clothes.

A message for adults

All the projects in Back-to-School Crafts have been designed for children to make, but occasionally they will need you to help. Some of the projects do require the use of sharp utensils, such as scissors or needles. Please read the instructions before your child starts work.

Making patterns

Follow these steps to make the patterns on pages 30 and 31. Using a pencil, trace the pattern onto tracing paper. If you're making a project out of fabric, you can cut out the tracing paper pattern and pin it onto the fabric. To cut the pattern out of cardboard, turn the tracing over, and lay it onto the cardboard. Rub firmly over the pattern with a pencil. The shape will appear on the cardboard. Cut out the shape.

When you have finished

Wash paintbrushes, and put everything away.

Put pens, pencils, paints, and glue in an old box or ice-cream container.

Keep scissors and any other sharp items in a safe place.

Stick needles and pins into a pincushion or a piece of scrap cloth.

BE SAFE

Look out for the safety boxes. They will appear whenever you need to ask an adult for help.

Ask an adult to help you use sharp scissors.

Bobble tree

This is a handy holder for hair bands, bobbles, and scrunchies. Why not make it in time for the new school year? Then you can get ready super-quick in the morning instead of hunting for your hair bands.

YOU WILL NEED

wooden mug tree	pale pink house paint
clear glue	paintbrush
small matchbox	plastic beads

1 Paint the mug tree pink. Let the first coat of paint dry (it will take about an hour), and then paint on a second coat.

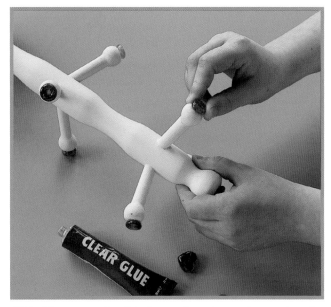

2 Glue on colorful plastic beads to the ends of the tree branches and to the base, leaving a space for the matchbox compartment.

3 Slide the matchbox apart, and paint the bottom section only with pink paint. Paint the inside and outside. Let the paint dry.

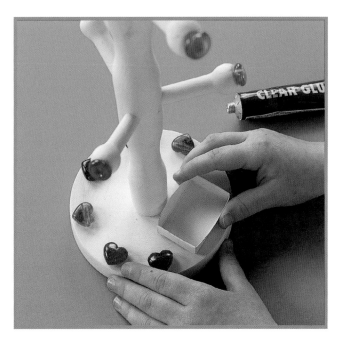

4 Glue the painted matchbox base to the mug tree stand as a little holder for clips.

Fold-up purse

Make a soft, sturdy purse from felt. This is an excellent fabric to use because you can glue it like paper—so there's hardly any sewing at all needed in this project.

YOU WILL NEED

purple and pink felt	needle and thread
sequins	scissors
glue	eraser
small button	chalk
ruler	

1 Cut out two pieces of purple felt, each 12in x 7½in (30cm x 19cm). Divide one piece of felt into thirds along the 12in (30cm) edge, and mark with chalk lines.

2 Cut two rectangles of pink felt 5¾in x 3in (14½cm x 7½cm). Cut out a third piece of pink felt 3¾in x 3in (9½cm x 7½cm)—this is a small pocket.

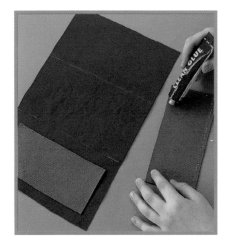

3 Glue the two large pink rectangles to the purple felt on either side. Glue on the pink pocket in the middle—remember not to glue along the top edge.

4 Now you are going to glue the second piece of purple felt to the back to make the purse thicker and sturdier. Before you stick the right-hand edges together, make a button loop. To do this, cut a small strip of purple felt. Loop it over and glue it down between the two purple sheets as shown.

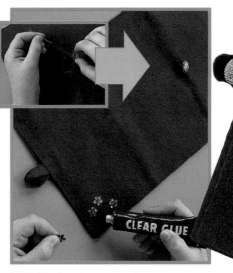

5 Cut out two strips of purple felt with wavy top edges, and glue them to the bottom of the pink sections on either side of the pocket. Cut a strip of purple felt to make the hankie holder, and glue it on either side of the large pink rectangle on the right, as shown. Fold your purse along the chalk lines, then erase the lines gently using a pencil eraser.

6 To finish, sew a button in place on the back of the purse in the middle of the second fold. Glue on sequins to decorate. You can attach keys to the pink felt sections using safety pins and slip a hankie under the felt bar.

Ask an adult to help you sew on the button.

9

Comic carton

Tidy away your comics into this brightly colored carton made from a cereal box. We've decorated ours with ribbed cardboard, which you can buy from a craft store.

YOU WILL NEED

yellow and green ribbed cardboard	ruler
	marker pen
empty cereal box	wide double-sided tape
	scissors

1 Using a ruler and marker pen, draw a line across the front of the cereal box. The line should go from the top and slant down to two-thirds of the way up one side, as shown.

2 Attach strips of double-sided tape to the four upright edges of the cereal box.

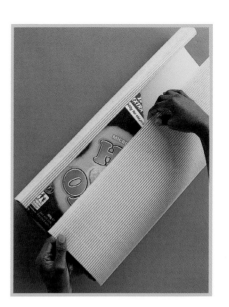

3 Place the yellow ribbed cardboard on the table with the ribbed side down. Peel off the backing paper from the double-sided tape, and lay the cereal box on the cardboard so the bottom edges line up. Wrap the cardboard around the cereal box.

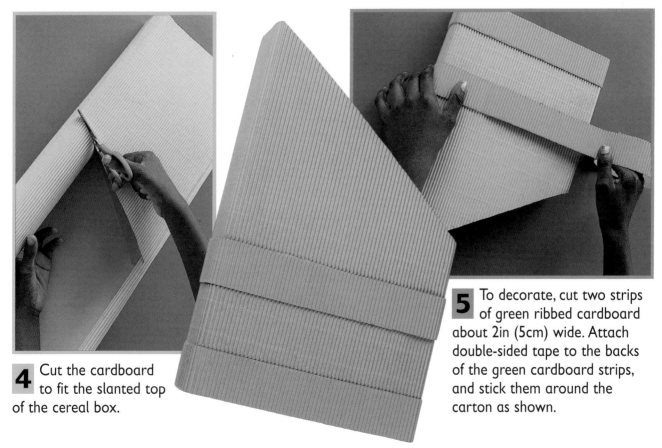

4 Cut the cardboard to fit the slanted top of the cereal box.

5 To decorate, cut two strips of green ribbed cardboard about 2in (5cm) wide. Attach double-sided tape to the backs of the green cardboard strips, and stick them around the carton as shown.

Pen cassette

Make this cool case for your pens out of an old video cassette box. It's simple to make and so practical—inside there's a weekly timetable for you to fill in and a small compartment for erasers.

YOU WILL NEED

video tape to draw around	patterned wrapping paper 9¾in x 8in (25cm x 20cm)
video box with a plastic cover	
self-adhesive craft foam	audio cassette box
magazines	pencil
scissors	blank postcard
felt-tip pens	alphabet stencil
glue	

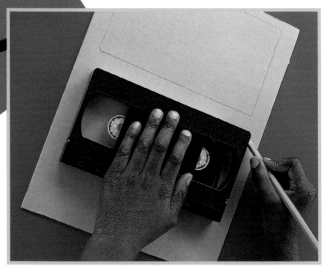

1 Draw around a video tape onto self-adhesive foam (draw onto the backing paper side of the foam). Draw around the tape again. Cut out the two foam rectangles.

12

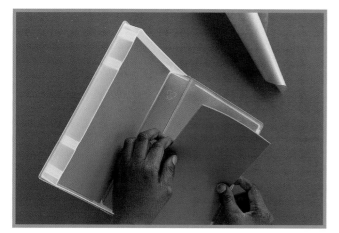

2 Peel off the backing, and stick the foam inside the lid and bottom of the video box.

3 Stencil a weekly timetable onto a postcard, and stick it inside the lid of the video box.

5 Glue the pictures onto the piece of patterned wrapping paper. You can stencil your name on, too. Slot the paper into the cover slip as shown.

6 Tape a magazine picture into the lid of an old audio cassette box. Put the box into your pen cassette to make a smaller compartment.

4 Carefully cut out pictures from a magazine—we've chosen racing cars.

School days chart

Use simple sewing to create this chart with pockets for each day of the week. Make picture cards to put in the pockets to remind you of what's coming up on each school day. You'll never forget your gym bag again!

YOU WILL NEED

- cotton fabric 18in x 19½in (46cm x 50cm) and a strip 4½in x 19½in (11cm x 50cm)
- red felt
- scissors
- ruler
- 5 plain white postcards
- all-purpose glue
- paper glue
- magazines
- needle and thread
- alphabet stencil
- black felt-tip pen
- pencil

1 Measure five 3-in (8½-cm) squares of red felt, and cut them out. Then measure a strip of felt 3in x 11in (8½cm x 28cm), and cut it out.

2 Stencil "M" for Monday on one square using a black felt-tip pen. Stencil letters onto the other squares for the rest of the week. Stencil "school chart" on the long strip of felt.

14

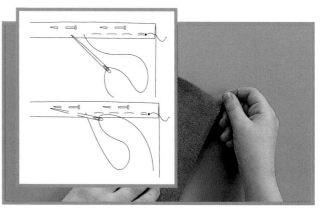

3 To neaten the edges of the cotton fabric, fold over a thin hem, and pin in place. Do this along the edges of both pieces of cotton fabric. This will also keep the fabric from fraying.

4 Now use a needle and thread to sew the hems. Use a simple running stitch (see diagram above), and take out the pins as you sew. You could ask an adult to machine sew the hems instead.

5 Place the fabric strip on top of the large piece of fabric so that it runs along the bottom (longer) edge. Pin the strip in place. Mark every 3¾in (10cm) along the strip with a pencil. Sew the strip in place along the edges (but not the top), and sew four upward lines at the 3¾in (10cm) marks to make the pockets. Glue the red felt squares above the pockets in the order of the week.

6 Cut out pictures from a magazine, or draw pictures to remind you what is happening at school each day. Trim the postcards so that they will fit into the pockets, and glue the pictures onto the postcards. Hang up your chart.

Ask an adult to help you use a sharp needle and pins.

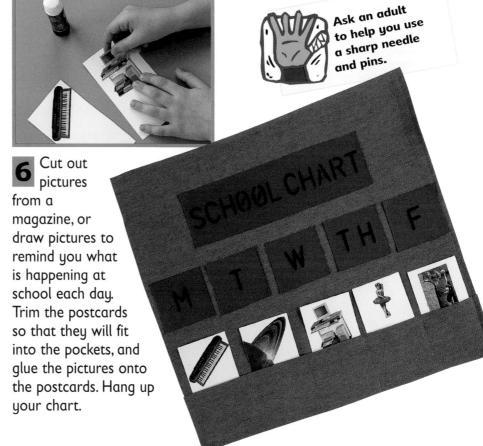

15

Pencil toppers

Make round or heart-shaped foam tops for your pens and pencils. They also make great back-to-school presents to give to your classmates— decorate each topper with a friend's initials.

YOU WILL NEED

red and blue craft foam	all-purpose glue
thin red ribbon	paintbrush
egg cup	alphabet stencil
pencil	
scissors	

1 Paste glue onto one side of a length of thin red ribbon. Wind the glued ribbon around a pencil. Cut off any extra ribbon left at the top.

2 Put a dab of glue on the flat top of the pencil. Stick on a length of red ribbon so the ends hang down. Put the pencil to one side to let the glue dry.

3 To make the topper, cut out two identical circles of blue craft foam. The best way to make circles is to draw around an egg cup.

4 Glue around the edge of one foam circle. Leave a gap where the pencil will go. Stick the two blue circles together.

5 Using an alphabet stencil, draw the first letter of your first name and the first letter of your second name onto red craft foam. Cut out the letters. Glue one to each side of the blue circle.

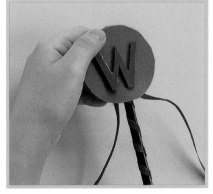

6 When the glue is dry, push the foam topper onto the end of the decorated pencil.

17

Rain-forest folder

This is a fun folder for schoolwork. There's a simple game on the cover, too—make snake counters for your friends so you can play it at break time.

1 Open the folder. Cut brown cardboard to cover the folder pocket exactly. Glue it on.

2 Cut out bush shapes from light and dark green cardboard. Stick the bush shapes onto the brown pocket so that they overlap. Leave a brown pathway as shown. Decorate the folder lid with green bushes, too.

3 Cut out exotic bird and insect pictures. We have used ready-made scraps, but you could cut them out of a magazine. Glue the pictures all over your folder but not on the brown pathway.

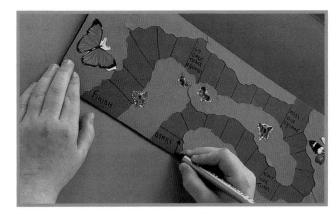

4 Draw steps on the path. Write instructions on some steps, such as "go back one place" or "miss a turn." Each player takes turns to throw dice and move his or her snake. The winner is the first player to reach the end of the path.

5 To make the snake counters, roll out a small snake from clay. Make ridge marks down its back with your fingernail. Roll up the tail into a spiral, and then bend up the neck. When the clay has dried, paint it a bright color. Make a few snake counters—one for each of your school friends.

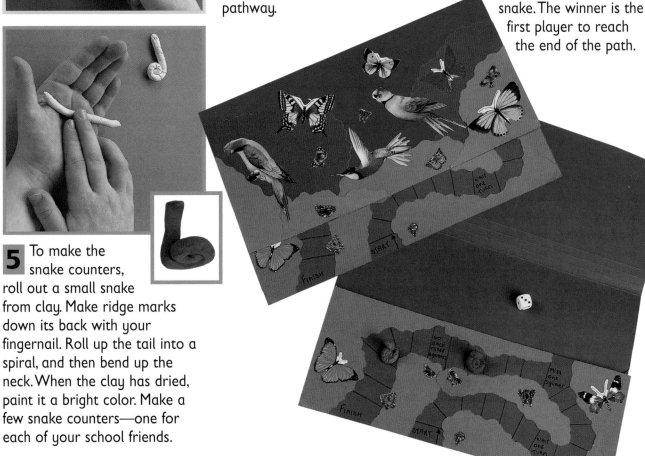

19

Pots for pens

To make this desk-top tidier, you'll need to search for a selection of cardboard tubes. Candies, chips, and some cheeses come in round boxes or tubes, so don't throw away the empty cartons.

1 Paint the cake base and the cardboard tubes with yellow paint. Let them dry.

20

2 Cut the scraps of wallpaper border into strips long enough to go around the cardboard tubes, and into different widths. Glue them around the tubes as shown.

3 Tape feathers inside the tubes at the top. Make sure that the feathers bend outward, not in toward the tube, or they will get in the way whenever you are putting your pens in.

4 Glue the decorated tubes in place on the cake base, with the taller ones for rulers and scissors at the back and wide, round containers for erasers and sharpeners at the front. Decorate your tube tidier with a toy—we've chosen a snake to go with our California desert theme.

Art tube

Make a bright holder for a big painting. Roll up your artwork, and slip it into the tube—it will fit snugly inside and won't fall out. You will need a big cardboard tube, so ask at a fabric store for a used cloth roll, or buy a poster tube from the post office.

YOU WILL NEED

cardboard tube 16in (40cm) long	scissors
	red poster paint
green felt	paintbrush
red felt	tracing paper
green ribbon	pins
narrow cord 55in (137cm) long	pencil
	white paper
glue	

1 Paint the outside of the cardboard tube with red poster paint. You may need two coats. Let the first one dry, and then paint again.

22

2 Glue green ribbon around both ends to give your tube a smart finish.

3 To make a felt pocket for a paintbrush, first trace the triangle pattern on page 30. Transfer the tracing onto paper, and cut out the template. Pin the template to the green felt, and cut out the triangle shape.

5 Cut out two rectangles of red felt, and glue them around the ends of the cord.

6 Now thread the cord through the tube, and knot the two ends together as shown to make a loop for carrying.

4 Put glue along the two long sides of the felt triangle. Hold your paintbrush against the poster tube, and stick the felt pocket down around it to make the pocket the correct size for your brush. Cut out three small circles of red felt, and glue them to the corners of the triangle. Hold the felt down while the glue dries.

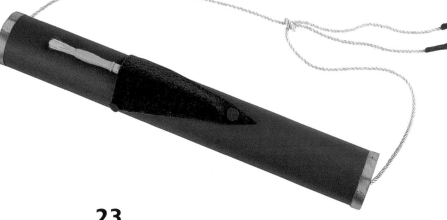

Keep-out kitten

At homework time keep little brothers and sisters out with this door hanger. There's a clock on the kitten's face so everyone knows how much peace and quiet you need to finish your assignment. Hush!

YOU WILL NEED

fluorescent pink and yellow cardboard

green cardboard

paper fastener

scissors

alphabet and number stencil

tracing paper

pencil

mug

darning needle

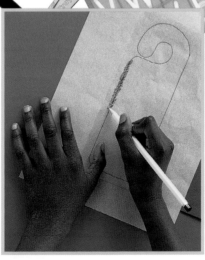

1 Trace the hook pattern on page 30. Cut the hook out of pink cardboard.

2 Draw around a mug onto yellow cardboard to make the cat's face. Draw on ears, eyes, nose, and whiskers. Make 12 marks around the face to form a clock. Cut out the cat.

24

3 Use the stencil to write a "Keep out!" or "Hush!" message on the door hanger. Then stencil numbers onto the cat clockface. You can just do 3, 6, 9, and 12.

4 Cut out 2 clock hands from green cardboard. One should be slightly shorter than the other.

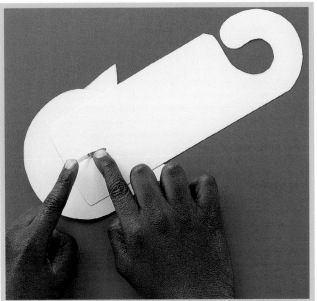

5 Make holes in the center of the clock, the ends of the hands, and the hanger (toward the bottom) using a darning needle. Join them together with a paper fastener. Press down the fastener legs on the back to keep it all together.

Ask an adult to help you make holes using the darning needle.

25

Activity apron

Here's a neat way to keep your school clothes clean when you're painting or crafting. Start by tracing the apron pattern on page 31. You can decorate the finished apron by gluing on felt shapes— we've added a flower.

YOU WILL NEED

19in x 28in (49cm x 72cm) piece of cotton fabric	large sheet of white paper
	pins
65in (164cm) length of binding	needle and thread
	scissors
tracing paper	pencil

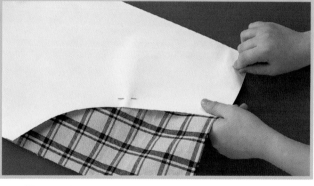

1 Trace the pattern on page 31. This pattern is in two parts. First trace the smaller shape in the middle, and transfer this tracing to the top of the white paper. Now trace the larger shape, and transfer it onto the paper, lining up the two parts along the dotted lines. Cut out the complete shape, but do not cut along the dotted line. Fold the cotton fabric in half lengthwise. Pin the paper pattern to the fabric, matching the top of the paper to the top of the fabric and the fold line to the fold in the fabric.

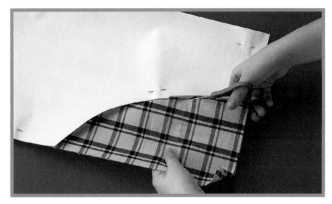

2 Cut the fabric along the curved edge of the template. This is the armhole of your apron.

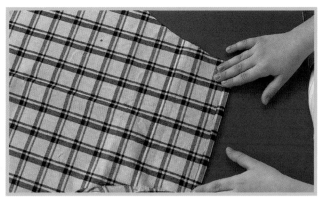

3 Unfold the fabric, and put it right-side down on the table. To keep the edges of the fabric from fraying, fold them over to make a hem, and pin the hem in place. Do this along every edge.

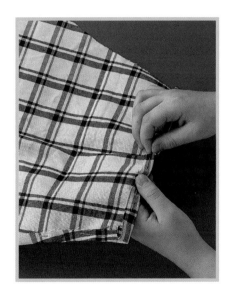

4 Using a simple running stitch (see the diagram on page 15), sew down the hem. Take out the pins as you sew. You could ask an adult to machine sew the hem instead.

Ask an adult to help you use a sharp needle and pins.

5 Cut a piece of binding 24in (60cm) long, and sew the ends to either side of the neck. Cut two pieces 20½in (52cm) long. Sew to each side of the apron.

27

Book snakes

These fat felt snakes are bookmarks for big reference books. When you're checking facts for a school assignment, you can use a book snake to keep your place in a chunky atlas or encyclopedia.

YOU WILL NEED

white paper

tracing paper

pencil

scissors

green felt for body

scraps of orange, black, and red felt

goggly eyes from a craft store

embroidery thread

needle

fabric glue

1 Trace the snake pattern on page 30. Transfer the tracing onto paper by following the instructions on page 5. Pin the paper template to a piece of green felt, and cut out a snake. Pin the template again, and cut out a second snake.

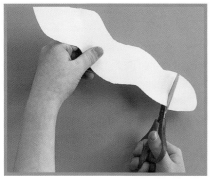

2 Cut the head off the paper template, and use the head template to cut out a snake head from green felt.

3 Trace the snake tongue from page 30, and use the tongue template to cut out a red felt tongue. Glue the tongue to the felt head, and glue one of the snake body shapes on top to cover up the tongue.

4 Turn the snake over, and glue goggly eyes to the head and colored felt spots to the body.

5 Sew the two snake bodies together at the tail with a few small stitches, one on top of the other. Ask an adult to help.

Ask an adult to help you use a sharp needle.

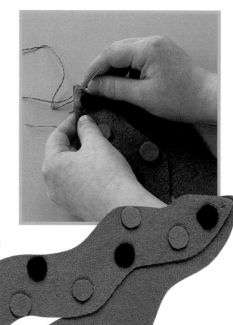

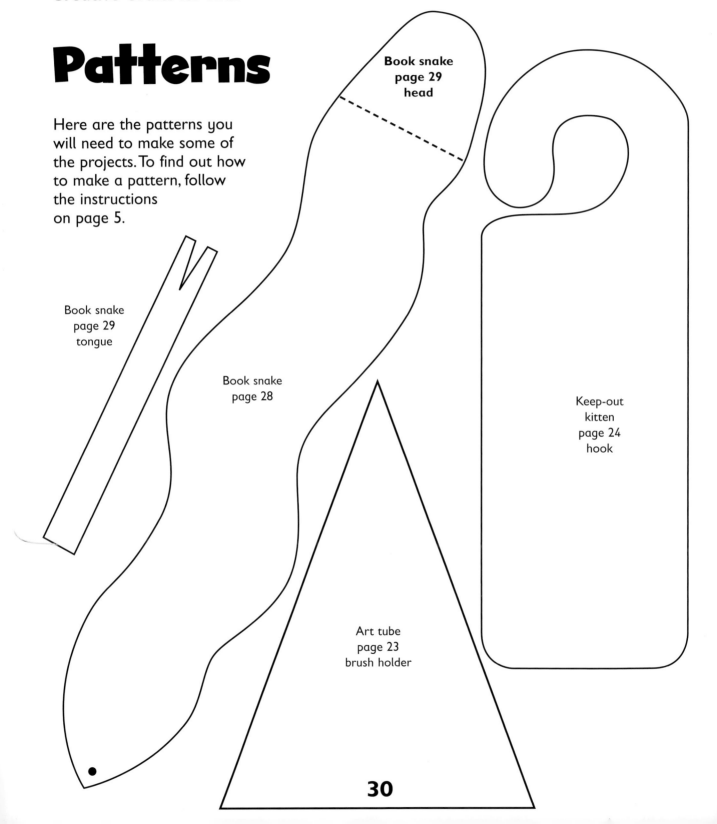

Patterns

Here are the patterns you will need to make some of the projects. To find out how to make a pattern, follow the instructions on page 5.

Book snake
page 29
head

Book snake
page 29
tongue

Book snake
page 28

Keep-out
kitten
page 24
hook

Art tube
page 23
brush holder

30

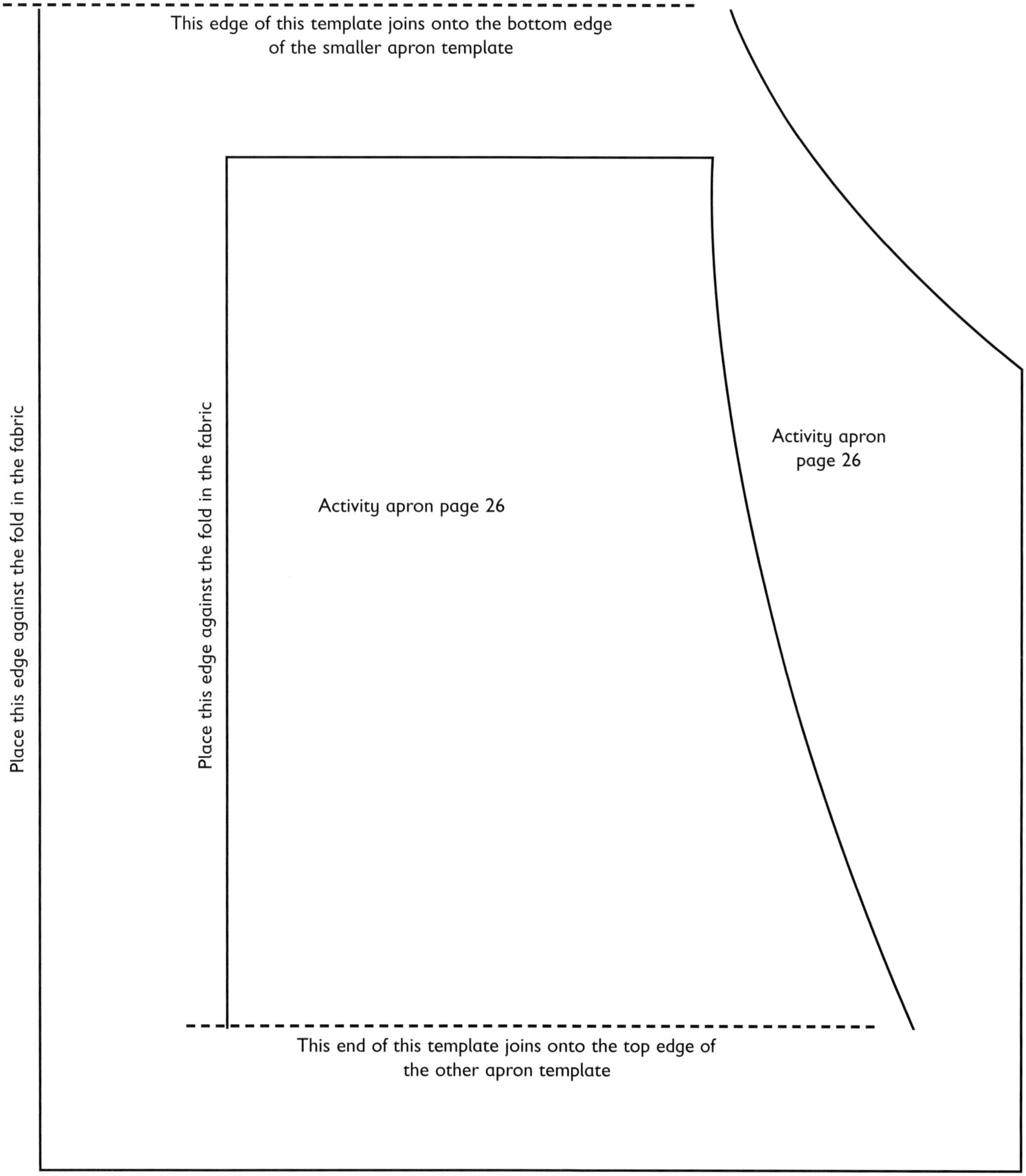

This edge of this template joins onto the bottom edge
of the smaller apron template

Place this edge against the fold in the fabric

Place this edge against the fold in the fabric

Activity apron page 26

Activity apron
page 26

This end of this template joins onto the top edge of
the other apron template

Glossary

atlas a book that contains maps and information about places

bobble a small object used as decoration

cassette a plastic case that contains audio or video tape

darning having to do with repairing holes in clothes

exotic unusual or colorful

goggly rolling or bulging, usually describing eyes

identical the same as or equal to

initial the first letter of a name

reference a source of information, such as an atlas or encyclopedia

scrunchie an elastic hair band covered with fabric

stencil to apply a design to a surface using a pattern

template a pattern from which similar things can be made

Index

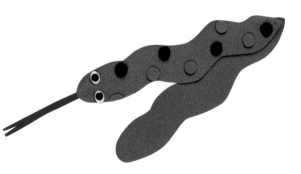